Military Animals

MINE-HUNTING ANIMALS

by Amy C. Rea

abdobooks.com

Published by Pop!, a division of ABDO, PO Box 398166, Minneapolis, Minnesota 55439. Copyright ©2022 by Abdo Consulting Group, Inc. International copyrights reserved in all countries. No part of this book may be reproduced in any form without written permission from the publisher. DiscoverRoo™ is a trademark and logo of Pop!.

Printed in the United States of America, North Mankato, Minnesota.

102021
012022

THIS BOOK CONTAINS RECYCLED MATERIALS

Cover Photo: US Navy
Interior Photos: US Navy, 1; Defense Visual Information Distribution Service, 5, 6, 8, 14, 15, 17, 23, 25, 29; US Department of Defense, 7, 24, 28; Eddie Worth/AP Images, 11; Denis Gray/AP Images, 12; Ville Palonen/Alamy, 18; Mary Hayes/AP Images, 20; iStockphoto, 21 (bee), 21 (dog), 21 (dolphin), 21 (rat), 21 (sea lion); Denis Poroy/AP Images, 27

Editor: Charly Haley
Series Designer: Laura Graphenteen

Library of Congress Control Number: 2020948853
Publisher's Cataloging-in-Publication Data
Names: Rea, Amy C., author.
Title: Mine-hunting animals / by Amy C. Rea
Description: Minneapolis, Minnesota : Pop!, 2022 | Series: Military animals | Includes online resources and index.
Identifiers: ISBN 9781532169977 (lib. bdg.) | ISBN 9781644945926 (pbk.) | ISBN 9781098240905 (ebook)
Subjects: LCSH: Animals--Juvenile literature. | Working animals--Juvenile literature. | Land mines--Juvenile literature. | Armed Forces--Juvenile literature. | Animals--War use--Juvenile literature.
Classification: DDC 355.424--dc23

WELCOME TO
DiscoverRoo!

Pop open this book and you'll find QR codes loaded with information, so you can learn even more!

Scan this code* and others like it while you read, or visit the website below to make this book pop!

popbooksonline.com/mine-hunting

*Scanning QR codes requires a web-enabled smart device with a QR code reader app and a camera.

TABLE OF CONTENTS

CHAPTER 1
Important Mine Hunters 4

CHAPTER 2
History 10

CHAPTER 3
Land Animals. .16

CHAPTER 4
Ocean Animals. 22

Making Connections. 30
Glossary 31
Index. 32
Online Resources 32

CHAPTER 1

IMPORTANT MINE HUNTERS

A **trainer** releases a dolphin from a boat. The dolphin and its trainer both work for the US Navy. The dolphin swims away into the ocean. It looks for a mine. It uses **sonar** to do this. The dolphin finds the

WATCH A VIDEO HERE!

mine in only 30 seconds! Then it swims back to the trainer. The trainer rewards the dolphin with a fish.

A US Navy officer treats a dolphin to some fish after a training exercise.

A dolphin finds a training sea mine during an exercise.

A mine is an **explosive**. Mines in the ocean can harm military ships or **submarines**. The US military trains dolphins to find mines before they can do any harm. These dolphins are part of the navy's **Marine** Mammal Program.

A practice explosion shows how dangerous mines can be.

The US military sometimes uses sea lions to find underwater mines.

When a dolphin uses sonar, it makes clicking sounds. When the sounds hit something, such as a mine, they bounce back to the dolphin. Dolphins can sense when something is metal and does not belong in the ocean. The dolphin puts a marker on the mine. Human navy swimmers will find it later.

Other animals help find mines too. Sea lions use their strong eyesight. Rats and dogs sniff around to smell mines. Even bees are used to find mines.

DID YOU KNOW? A trained rat can find all the mines in a 2,000-square-foot (185-sq-m) area in 20 minutes. It would take a human four days to do that.

CHAPTER 2

HISTORY

The US military started using dogs for mine hunting in 1943. The dogs could find mines while training. But they became distracted on the battlefield. The military found new ways to train

LEARN MORE HERE!

Soldiers used mine-hunting dogs during World War II (1939–1945).

the dogs. Eventually the dogs became good at their jobs. In 1989, the military began a program in Afghanistan for mine-hunting dogs. That program started with only 16 dogs but grew to more than 100.

Rats have been trained to hunt for mines in several countries, including this rat in Cambodia.

The US Navy began its **Marine Mammal Program** in 1960. It started by studying and training dolphins. It later added sea lions. The animals find mines and do other jobs.

In 2000, researchers in Tanzania started training rats to find mines. A few years later, a university in Croatia found that honeybees could be trained for mine hunting as well.

 **DID YOU KNOW?** In the 1980s, the Marine Mammal Program had more than 100 dolphins.

TIMELINE

1943
The US military begins using dogs to find mines.

1960
The US Navy opens its Marine Mammal Program.

1960
The US Navy begins studying dolphins to see if they can find mines.

2000
Researchers train rats to find mines.

2007
Researchers discover that honeybees can be trained to find mines.

2019
The US military works on making robots to eventually replace mine-hunting dolphins.

CHAPTER 3
LAND ANIMALS

Land mines can still explode years after they are buried. That is why it is important to find and remove them.

Dogs can smell both metal and plastic mines. They can even sniff out

COMPLETE AN ACTIVITY HERE!

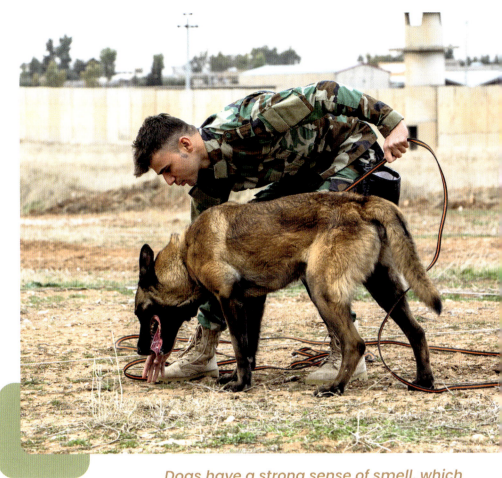

Dogs have a strong sense of smell, which helps them find mines.

mines in soil that has a lot of metal in it.

Dogs can also go into areas that are hard for humans to reach.

Trainers use food to get mine-hunting rats to work.

Rats also use their sense of smell to find mines. They have helped militaries in several countries, including Cambodia and Mozambique. Both countries have lots of mines still buried from past wars.

The rats are trained to scratch at spots that smell like **explosives**. A rat is hooked up to a **harness**. It walks through a field of mines. When the rat finds a mine, a **trainer** rewards it with food.

> **DID YOU KNOW?**
>
> **Rats are light enough to walk over mines without making the mines explode.**

Bees cover a mine that is filled with syrup.

Bees can also sniff out mines. Trainers put traces of explosives into syrup for honeybees to smell. The bees learn to think of food when they smell the explosive. They fly toward mines that have the same smell.

HOW DO ANIMALS FIND MINES?

CHAPTER 4

OCEAN ANIMALS

Militaries often use dolphins and other ocean animals to find mines. Dolphins can locate objects that are floating in the water or buried in the ocean floor. In this way, dolphins can find dangerous mines.

LEARN MORE HERE!

Like all members of the military, mine-hunting dolphins need training.

Navy sailors practice destroying a mine.

Navy sailors are always nearby as the dolphins work. The sailors make sure the dolphins stay safe and focused.

24

Military members and dolphins train together in the Gulf of Mexico.

When a dolphin finds a mine, it marks the mine with a **transponder**. This tool sends a signal to navy sailors. The sailors follow the signal and find the mine. Then they can safely destroy the mine.

DID YOU KNOW? Military dolphins need two to three years of training before they can begin working.

ROBOTS

Scientists have created robots that can find mines in the ocean. One day these mines may replace dolphins and sea lions. These robots are less expensive than animals. And robots can tell what kind of mine they find. Animals can only show that they found a mine. Knowing more about the kind of mine helps militaries plan how to handle it.

Sea lions use their good eyesight to find mines. The sea lion holds a **clamp** in its mouth and attaches it to an object in the water. Then navy sailors can pull the object in. If the object is a mine, the sailors will safely destroy it.

A navy sailor hands a sea lion a clamp. The clamp is used to mark mines.

A group of dolphins swims ahead of a military ship.

Mines can harm ships. They can hurt people. That is why it is important for military animals to find them.

Mine-hunting animals have skills that people do not. They can find mines more safely and quickly than people can.

These animals help militaries protect

people around the world.

Military animals save people's lives by finding dangerous mines.

MAKING CONNECTIONS

TEXT-TO-SELF

Militaries studied animals to learn how they could be used to find mines. What would you like to learn about animals?

TEXT-TO-TEXT

Have you read other books about military animals? How were those animals similar to or different from the ones described in this book?

TEXT-TO-WORLD

Mine hunting is just one job that animals can do. Have you ever seen an animal working with people? What kind of animal was it? What was it doing?

GLOSSARY

clamp — something that presses two or more parts together and holds them firmly.

explosive — something that causes an explosion, or a loud and dangerous breaking apart of things.

harness — a vest or strap that wraps tightly to an animal's body.

marine — related to the ocean.

sonar — in biology, the method of echolocation used in air or water by animals such as bats or dolphins. Animals do this to learn about where they are and what is around them by making sounds and listening to how they bounce back.

submarine — a ship that travels underwater.

trainer — a person who teaches animals.

transponder — something that can send out a signal.

INDEX

bees, 9, 13, 15, 20

dogs, 9, 10–11, 14, 16–17

dolphins, 4–9, 13, 14, 15, 22–25, 26

navy, 4, 7, 9, 13, 14, 24–26

rats, 9, 13, 15, 19

sea lions, 9, 13, 26

ships, 6, 28

sonar, 4, 8

submarines, 6

ONLINE RESOURCES
popbooksonline.com

Scan this code* and others like it while you read, or visit the website below to make this book pop!

popbooksonline.com/mine-hunting

*Scanning QR codes requires a web-enabled smart device with a QR code reader app and a camera.